ALSO BY DAVID GARRIGUES

Ashtanga Yoga for Beginners

Vayu Siddhi: Secrets to Yogic Breathing

Maps and Musings

Teaching Yoga with Verbal Cues

Graphic design/layout by *Jesse Molina* (awakecreativestudio.com) | Cover design by *Rob Court* with redesigned elements by *Jesse Molina*. | Asana illustrations by *Bill Ross* | ISBN: 978-1-7375354-2-3

Ecstatic Discipline

46 Poems for Lovers of Hatha Yoga

DAVID GARRIGUES
EDITED BY JOY MARZEC

1

I'm a Simple Man.

If I don't find virtue,
beauty,
nobility,
dignity,
and truth in my pose
       I will not find them elsewhere.
That is why practice is everything,
holds everything,
reveals everything to me.

I told you,
I am a Simple Man.

Try to tell me that doing asanas is only
       physical exercise and I stopper up my ears
            like Nandi does when anyone utters a
            word against his beloved Shiva.

"Asana Vidya Ki Jai!"

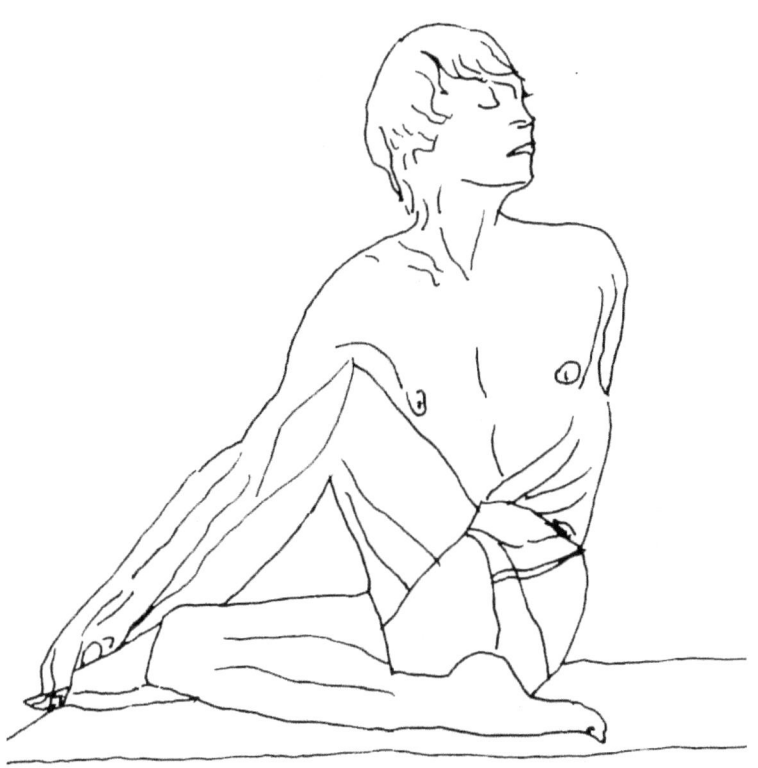

2

Your asanas are the sporting angels
        that you wrestle with in a mortal struggle
            to realize the noble desires
                housed in your secret soul.
But don't expect the floodgates of Nirvana
        to open easily for you.
These angel asanas don't let just anyone in.
You've got to prove your mettle day after day.

Sukham—Ease,
as in your asana is to be "Steady and Agreeable"
        is hard won.
Those asanas are mighty wrestlers
        who insist that you show up and fight.

They parry your every hold,
move,
or strategy.
They'll pin you to the ground
        while barely lifting a finger
            and then refuse your surrender.

As you battle and develop skill,
the asana angels stand beside you and show you
    there is more Sthira and Sukha to be had.

When you go up against these great opponents:
Triangle,
Bound Angle,
All Limbs,
Tree,
there's no resting,
no standing on the podium,
no exhausting what can be learned.

But being defeated by them in the ring each day
    makes you strong,
fit for admittance to the high-pinnacled peaks
    where your ego disappears.

The noise in your head is quieted.
You become immersed in the quest to know
    why you were born.
Dead to things that don't matter.
Riotously alive to things that do matter.

3

Dear one,
Go off by yourself and sit down.

Contemplate the largest scope,
the highest of the high,
and do this for yourself:
decide what your duty is.

Don't let anyone else decide for you.

In your secret heart,
what are you here for?

4

During these precious moments of practice
    I reduce my mundane needs.
I temporarily turn away from material concerns.
I withdraw my attention into the confines of my body
    to conduct an inward quest for Self Knowledge.
This is the essence of all practice.
To empty out.
To come to stillness and silence.
To see the sacred that exists beyond my thoughts,
beyond the false appearance of the ordinary world.

5

I often find myself giving an ultimatum
       to the Great Spirit.

I stand at the front door of myself and demand,
"I have to do these poses in this order…or else!"
But I soon shake my head.
Silly ultimatums never get me anywhere.
The truth is I have no demands.

No!
Quite the opposite!
I come to the door where the great art
       is taking place as a beggar.
I plead to gain admittance on any terms.

I bang on the door crying,
"Let me in!
I'll be weak,
stiff,
unbendable,
challenged in every way.
Just open the door!

Let me step on the magic carpet and do anything at all.
A simple clear breath will do.
A mighty arm reach.
Scooping my belly after flushing the air out of my lungs.
Please!
These are plenty for me!!"

When the door opens,
it turns out lil ol' broken down David
      gets renewed quite easily
           if I drop all of my ridiculous agendas.
Yes,
my hilarious agendas.

6

Why is Mula Bandha so important?
Because it brings you to the root of your spine,
and awakens you to the Most Glorious Axis,
the source of all vitality.

Why is Uddhyana Bandha so important?
Because it does almost the same thing
but it is far easier to do.

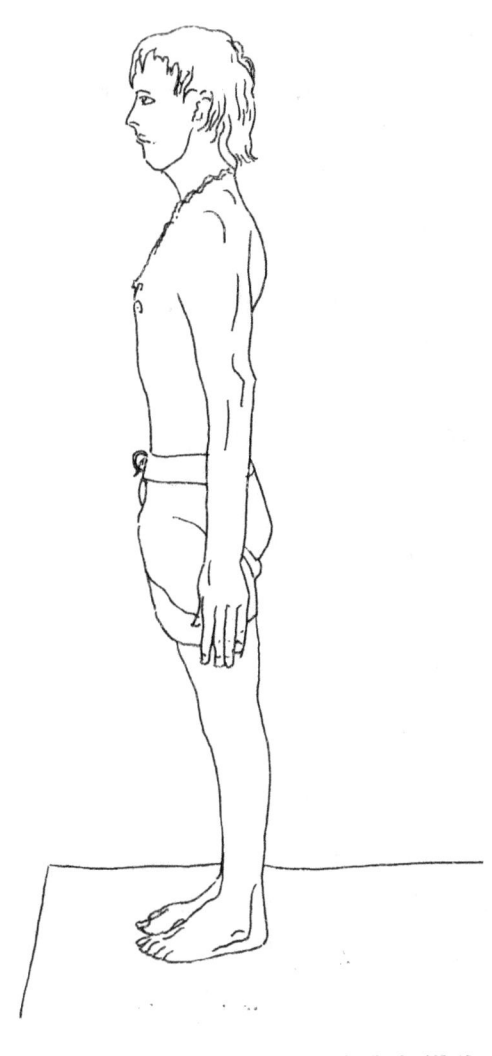

7

They say when the student is ready the teacher appears.
I must be ready because I have a new teacher!
A massive centuries old tree that I can see and
    commune with from my backyard yoga cave.

I wrote a poem for you old tree.
My tree displays the root qualities of Self:
    SAT – EXISTENCE
    CIT – CONSCIOUSNESS
    ANANDA — BLISS

There it stands alone.
Rooted.
Massive.
Tall.
Boldly proclaiming,
"I AM!"

Every tiniest part of this giant is awake
    and absorbing every nuance.
Pure riotous joy exudes from each cell and shoots forth
    into the cosmos with astounding force.

I will never again say that a tree can't know joy.
I aim to be like my tree!

8

Close the gates of your eyes.
See visions meant for you.

Stop up your ears.
Take to the inner sounds.
Practice inner listening.
Hear stories meant for you.

Empty your mouth cave.
Expand into your interior vastness.
Discern unique truths
      and sublime insights meant for you.
Awaken to your skin's envelope and feel alive
      in an original way meant for you.

Use your hatha yoga skill to create a Maha Mudra,
a psychic vessel of containment,
that opens you to the marvelous inward state.

Soon you'll know how to do your sacred work.
Soon you'll share yourself with this world.

9

Dear Yogi,
Feeling dark?
Do a backbend.

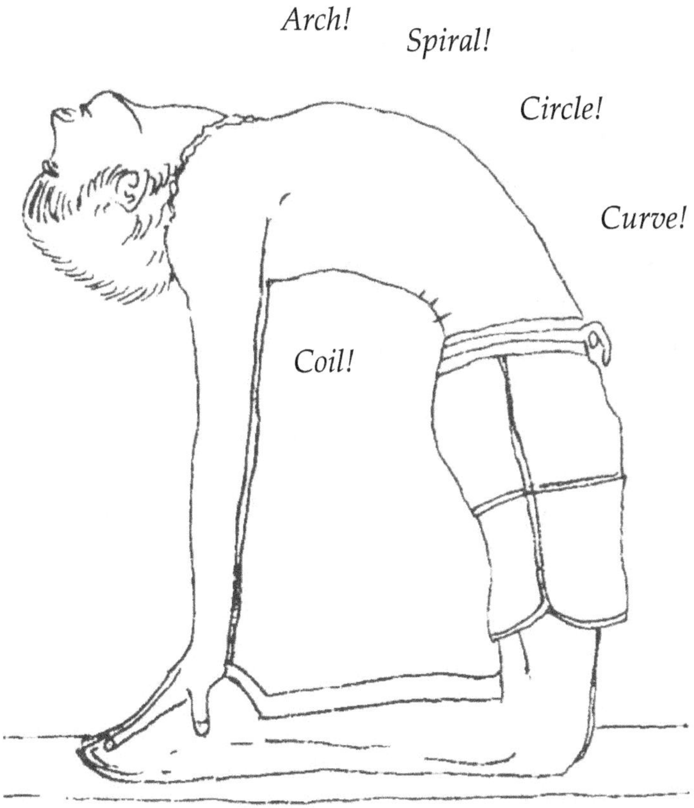

Arch! *Spiral!*

Circle!

Curve!

Coil!

10

Success in practice only needs three ingredients:
Consistency — Longevity — Sincerity.

Notice that the words perfect or intense are absent
    from this basic recipe.
There may be phases when you are intense
    and you even catch glimpses of perfection,
but what about when you are not as intense,
or don't improve,
or skill eludes you,
or it is painfully obvious that you are less than perfect?

Success is still yours if you keep going.
Show up each day and be sincere.
That is all.

Doggedly do your best within your circumstances
    and you'll find out that you are better for it,
better for yoking yourself to the discipline of yoga.

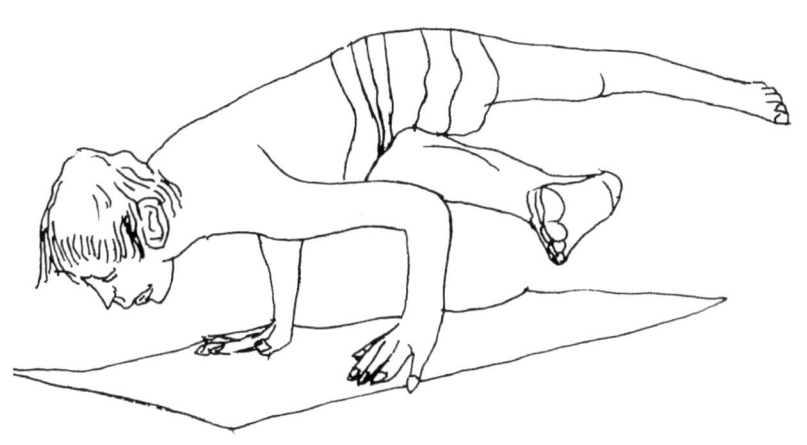

11

You want to know what pulled me through those beginning hard years of teaching?

My unwavering belief in the healing power of yoga.

12

I've long known about an old remedy for pain,
where the Indigenous would take a child
    who was acting out down to the icy cold
        stream for a dunk.
Encountering the stark face of reality
    like a slap in the face
        will put you right.

I use this remedy on myself daily.
The cold dunk of ujjayi breathing,
bandhas,
vinyasa,
and dristi,
is exactly what I need to set my spirit right,
to set my spirit straight.

David says:
I'll do whatever it takes to remember that I'm always
    surrounded by the magic of existence.

13

Be like the bhakti poet Mira who said,
"Be mad with love though no one can see."

People won't understand you.
They won't get you.
It doesn't matter.

Fight on!

Make your own grand parade
      for an audience of one.
Fully amuse yourself.
Be a legend in your own mind.

Create and create
      for yourself and by yourself.
Open up whole solitary worlds
      that no one else will visit but you.

Be your own best friend,
your biggest supporter,
your most vocal cheerleader.

Don't wait for others to like or get what you do.

Create whole worlds in your own image
        and thoroughly enjoy yourself doing it.

14

It's cold.
I'm old.
Just getting out of bed is bold.
But I do like the ancients told
    to be part of the yogi fold.
Fear or inertia ain't gonna take hold.
I do what it takes to break that mold.
Renew and be part of the yogi fold.
Join the yogi fold.

15

It's a fact that daily practice is hard.
It doesn't matter how you spin it.
No pep talk,
inspiration,
or effortlessness can eliminate it.
There's nothing to take away the daily encounter
    with difficulty and obstacles.

But knowing this fact lightens the burden a bit,
you don't have to think there's something wrong
    when you struggle.
It's not your mind playing tricks on you.
It's not your attitude.
It's not that you don't love it enough.
You're simply fighting the good fight each day
    like any good yogi doing their duty.

16

Do you realize there are trillions upon trillions of ways
  to explore the Primary Series?

It's your practice.
No one can do it for you.
Praise the Lord!

17

Dec 24th,
2020.
4:30am.
41 degrees.
Backyard temple.

Hatha yoga,
and my Allies,
Prithivi the Earth,
Indra the Sky,
and Chandra the Moon,
are all here.

I salute the predawn
     with my body Yantras and skillful breath.
The air is cold and fresh.

Vayu the God of Wind,
gives me a caress
     --a SVAHA--
          an AMEN to my face
              and off we go!

Gone to Samadhi,
gone to celebrate You!
We!
I!
They!
It!
The whole lot!
The whole magical show!

All of us,
crazy,
wonderful,
loving,
wild beings who have been thrown together
      to share this supreme world
           during COVID-19.
Christ Mass Eve!!

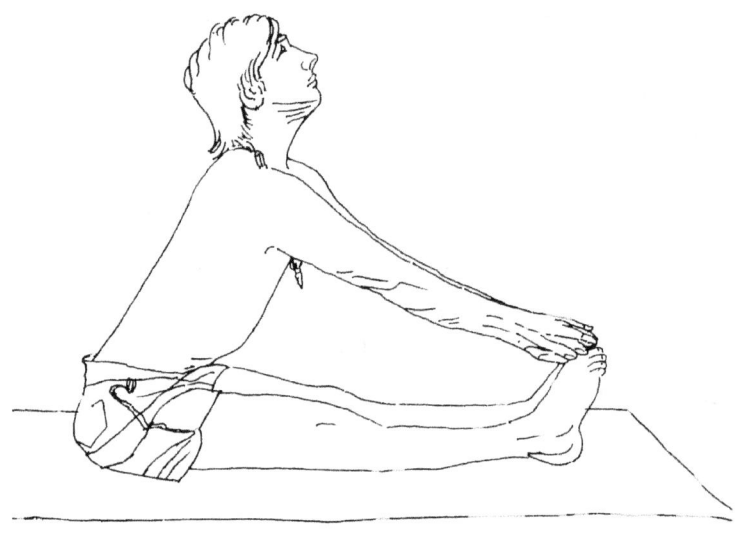

18

For me,
Yoga is a shared experience even though
    I practice in solitude.
Every morning I commune with
    all the other fellow seekers,
lovers of the invisible Oneness.

One cannot do yoga alone because yoga is the
attempt to join with all,
to consider all,
to live for all.

There's no isolation in yoga.
No "I" and "You".
No other.
No enemy.
No "I".
No "Me"
No "Mine".
No fear of others.
Yoga is solidarity with all life.

19

I used to not relate to those ugly gargoyles
  on the outside of churches.
I resisted the sentinels,
so terrible looking and menacing.

But in these tough times,
I see the necessity for having such fierce guardians to
  protect the inner sanctuary.
I need potent forces to protect my body temple,
to guard my spirit,
and help me remember soul.
In my postures,
I've taken to setting up my own gargoyles.
I protect myself with those same terrible faces
  and scare tactics to ward off evil spirits.

I put on my mean face,
show my mind that I am serious.
I'm not above repeatedly stamping the ground with
  my feet like a mad moose readying to charge.
I'll stick out my tongue,
bug out my eyes,
power up my limbs,

and let out a growling roar like a hungry lion if it
      helps me to take charge for real
            and get on with doing the do.

Sometimes tapas needs to become catharsis.
Exercise needs to become exorcism.

The sucking whirlpool of despair
      won't suck me down.
I take no guff,
no nonsense.
I expel the demons,
fear,
panic,
worry,
and wrath.

On the outside I look like the ugly gargoyle
      but on the inside the horrible tension melts
           away and the stifling fear is gone.

My inner foxhole once again becomes a refuge.
I win through to the healing balm of tenderness.

20

How challenging should you make each pose?
Make it hard enough to be catapulted
    into the present moment.

Then drop your grudges
    and become receptive
        to loving and being loved.

21

Relentless practice.
That's my answer to everything.
Sorry if that sounds extreme.
But *relentless practice* is where I work out
     my troubles alone (thank goodness).

Returning to my prayer rug
     and offering myself to asanas,
breathing,
and absorption,
works wonders against my nagging woes.

Instead of lashing out or blaming others for my pain,
I lean on no one but the great allies that have been
       gifted to me from heaven:
my breath,
my limbs,
my spine,
my consciousness,
my spirit.

David says:
Relentless practice is my preventative medicine.
It keeps me in form.
Keeps me knowing beauty.
Keeps me being generous.
Keeps me walking about thankful.

```
    R
        E
            L
                E
                    N
                        T
                            L
                                E
                                    S
                                        S
    P   R   A   C   T   I   C   E
```

22

There might be billions of ways to spin it
       but only one thing ever really matters:
being riotously awake like the Mad Holy Goof.

The Mad Holy Goof knows
       the noble love of existence.
The Mad Holy Goof is fully in this rapture now.
The Mad Holy Goof is forever a trickster.
The Mad Holy Goof dodges demons and forgets
       the past and future with wily dexterity.

Mad Holy Goof,
where are you?

Mad Holy Goof,
stand up inside of me.

Mad Holy Goof,
don't ever leave me.

Mad Holy Goof,
David bows to you.

23

Even when the entire world seems to be screaming,
"No!"
There,
behind the human's necessary agonies
      of protests and suffering,
is OM resounding,
"Yes!"

24

Naysayers,
those who disapprove of you and what you love,
will come from all corners;
inner and outer,
near and far,
above and below,
on either side,
day and night,
before and after,
or maybe seated right next to you at the dinner table.

Oh well,
never mind the Naysayers.

Simply say,
"YES,"
to your truth.

Never stop saying,
"YES,"
to your truth.

25

When it comes to doing an asana,
5 breaths duration is not enough for me.

I'm more like a hermit crab.
I set up shop in that shell.
That shape becomes my home and refuge.

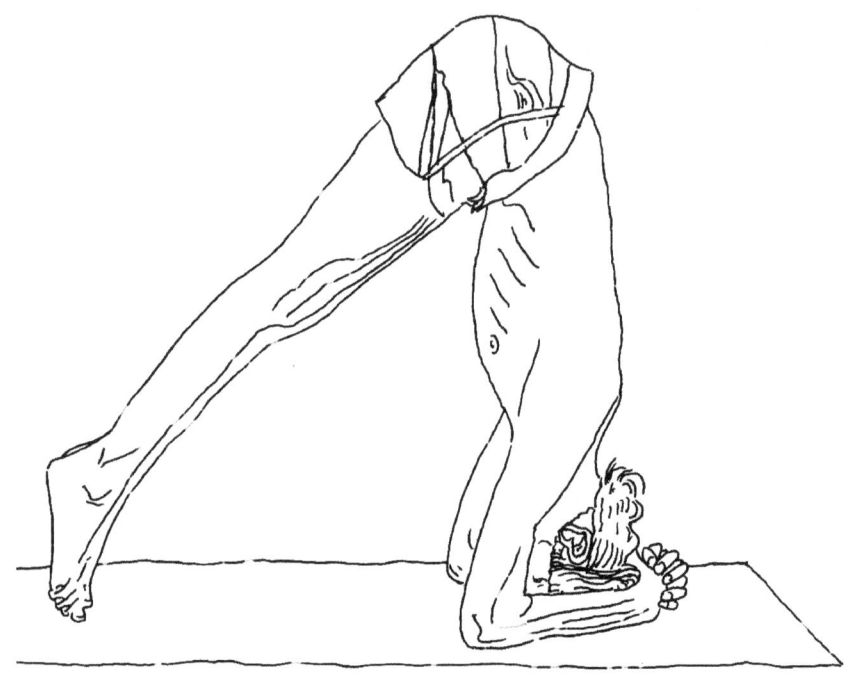

26

"When the going gets tough, the Tough get going."

It's a trite quote,
I know,
but it's suitable for the yogi who trains all the time
 to carry a heavy load.
When others are wilting,
drowning under pressure,
the yogi is ready to be a rock steady presence
 and bear the weight of staying constant.

We can't all crumble,
be taken down,
grow silent or withdraw.
Let the yogi in you be that someone.

Be a plain loving presence who does
 what needs to be done in a good spirit.
Be there for yourself,
your loved ones,
and others.
Fight the fight one day at a time.

The Great Spirit will move within you
 if you keep stepping forward.

27

Hey!
You!
Student!

Is it so hard to accept that the universe is
 asking you to do something beautiful?

Okay then,
let's get on with it.

28

I'm a hatha yoga musician.
My body is the band that makes my asana songs.

My arms and legs play bass,
supplying the earth
 and eloquently laying down the heavy,
funky foundation.

My senses play guitar,
nimbly picking out the
 ripping-rippling-charging-soaring melodies.

My spine is the lead singer,
extending - flexing - twisting,
launching a passionate - mighty ranged-
 fearless voice out into space.

My breath is the drummer,
who uses the diaphragm and lungs as his kit.
He delicately taps and radically pounds out the
 endlessly varied rhythms.

My palate is the conductor,
who surveys the entirety
 from the raised pulpit inside my head,

and makes a unified ensemble
        out of the disparate cast.

So many other players are part of this great Yantra,
each contributing their original sounds and
        adding to the glorious rocking
              devotional asana symphony.

Each pose is a new song,
a praise that chases away restlessness,
lethargy,
fears,
sadness,
or at least gives me respite from my pains.

There are many quiet refrains,
many rests,
and silences between the notes.

There are also many jubilant hallelujahs
        and jumps
               and shouts for joy.

It's asana music I live for.
It's yoga freedom I love.

29

On the first day of creation,
Trickster the Great Magician
    who set up this world said,
"HUMANS WILL ALWAYS BE GAMBLING."

The fact that gambling comes with being born
    and getting a face could be bad news
        but walking the razor's edge
            is a great delight to the yogi.

You say:
"If I'm always risking,
then let me take control over my choices.
Let me gamble with gusto and reach for what I cherish most.
Let me go for it boldly,
openly,
trustingly.
I'll try my best to risk on my own terms.
I'll continue to roll the dice even when repeated
    failures occur.

Eventually my lack of skill will become skill.
Eventually I'll shape my destiny.
Eventually the great secret vision in my heart
   will bear fruit,
at least in ways seen fit by Trickster,
who made us all and attached us to this
   wild ecstatic game."

O yogi,
embrace being a gambler.
Summon your courage,
faith,
and bet on the highest stake of all:

> **your**
> **abililty**
> **to**
> **befriend**
> **the**
> **Secret One!**

30

You develop powers by practicing asana.
They
     are
          called
               Siddhis:

Leg power!
Arm power!
Spine Power!
Belly power!
Breath power!
Digestive power!
Intellect power!
Discernment power!
Creative power!
Mind Control power!
Restraining power!
Enjoyment power!

Earth power!
Water power!
Fire power!
Air power!
Space power!
Stillness power!
Emptiness power!

But it all amounts to very little if you can't
 answer this question,
"How will I wield all this power?"

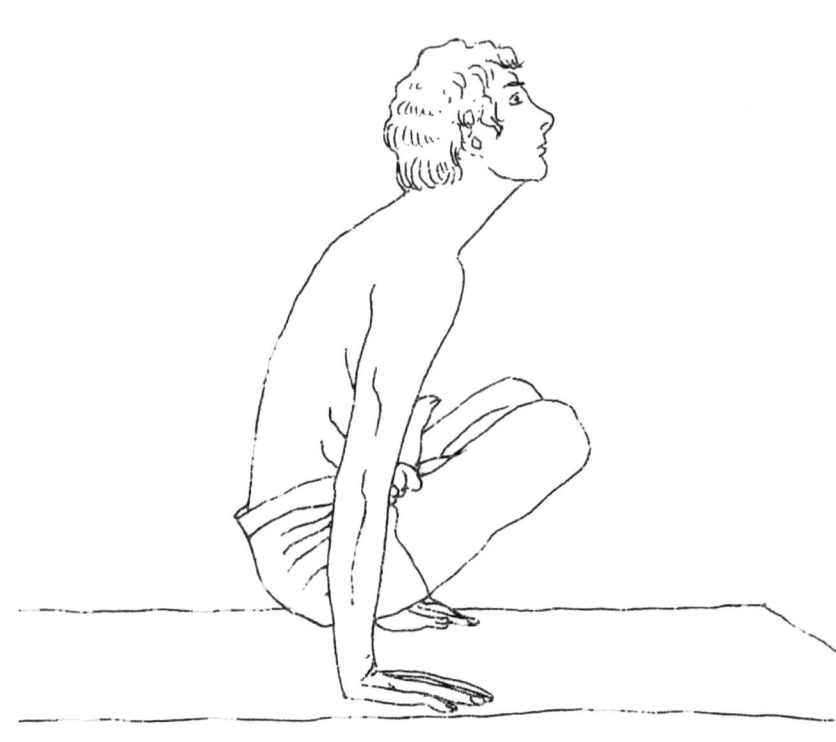

31

I give myself the freedom and space
    to perfect my pose.

Yes,
I know the word PERFECT is disliked these days
    but listen to my definition of perfect:
To be involved in a lively process of playful work.
When I pursue perfection it isn't to get a final result.
No!
I don't want that deadly and dismal trap.
I aim to explore endlessly,
to exercise my curiosity without limit,
to enjoy my interest and follow my fascination.

Sure,
I like it when I improve
    but I don't actually need to improve.
Possibilities are what I need.
To have as many attempts in as many ways
    as my heart desires.

This is what perfection means to me.
This is the gift David gives himself everyday.

32

I don't know my father well because
 he left when I was 7.
I guess he didn't want to be a part of my life.

My memories of us together are few
 but I can recall one.
He called me by the nickname of *Weed*
 because I was growing so fast.
Now that could be an insult!
I mean who wants to be called *Weed?!*
And yet,
I have taken that name far.

In my life,
I'm that pesky guy who refuses to lose.
I'm gonna grow
 and grow
  and keep growing
   just like a Morning Glory.

You can subject me to all manner of hardship,
deprivation,
obstacle,
challenge,
set back,
poison,
and I'll keep right on fighting.
Winning through.
Blossoming.

I find soul expression
 where others might wither or give up.

33

On your yoga journey
    you will come to a tipping point.

Suddenly,
staying in the asana will sound better
    than floating through to the next posture.

You'll be drawn to stillness
    (and not because you are tired)
        but from your soul's thirst
            for the depths of consciousness.

You'll tire of movement
    like a chocolatier tires of chocolate.

Perhaps you doubt me?
But it will happen
    if the Goddesses and Gods smile upon you.

34

Just being in a pose is bold,
audacious,
courageous!

David in Down Dog announces to the cosmos and
 all its inhabitants,
"I will commune with the Sacred Unseen Friend."

35

Oh my mind,
a riddle for you to chew on.

It is only when you have maximum self-acceptance
    that you can be continuously dissatisfied,
and being continually dissatisfied
    is essential to self acceptance.

Thus,
self-acceptance is not a condition
    where you're satisfied with yourself,
and being dissatisfied is not a condition
    where you don't accept yourself.

When both qualities are present
    in their strongest measure
        then work can happen.
Yoga can happen.
Knowledge can arrive.

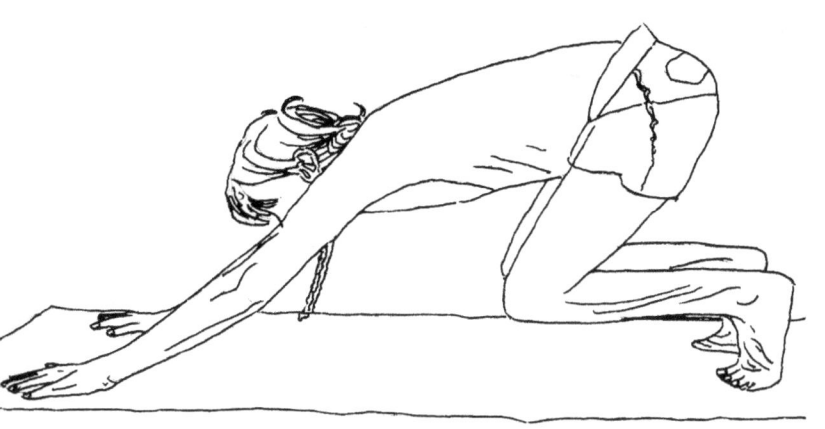

36

Behind the layers of the unoriginal me,
the copycat follower
      who doesn't think for himself,
is my own view!
Backbending tapas gives me the Shakti
      to perceive the world with my own eyes.
By arching my back I gain the strength,
flexibility,
stamina,
and heart to use my own voice.

I'm only a backbend away from sharing
      my truth with the world.

37

Expulsion of darkness requires David to know
    when to strike with the battle axe of dynamism
    or when his best weapons are
        softness and tenderness.

38

My anger is so often with me
    that I make the best of it.
I've learned to use it to rail against my despair
    and to fight back against complacency.

Anger helps me to win the battle
    of getting out of bed and onto my mat
        especially as the months
            and years pile up.

I use anger to scatter unworthy thoughts
    that don't belong in my head,
and kick them out using decisive force.

Discipline?
I win it by sipping my anger
    like it's the sweetest elixir.

Darkness or giving up?
Being overwhelmed - fearful - frozen?
I combat all of these with positive action
    that is fueled by anger.

Sometimes strength comes to me only
    when I finally get mad enough to push against
        my weaknesses time and again.
My anger is only something to fear
    if I don't listen to it and respond to it.

When I channel my anger,
honor my anger,
own my anger,
befriend my anger,
give voice to my anger,
express my anger with love,
a far greater world opens before me.

A favorite quote from the Yoga Vashista says:
"By the application of highest action
    to the point of gnashing one's teeth,
impurity is overcome by purity,
and action of the past is conquered."

39

Living while turning a blind eye to Spirit
    is like being caught in the coils
        of a mighty python who is getting ready
            to squeeze the life out of me
                and eat me.
As I am threatening the snake,
saying with perfect assurance
    that I am going to wrestle it to the ground
        and go on about my way,
my life is slipping away
    or worse I'm already dead.

40

Ode to Utkatasana!

I was 26 when I first laid eyes on Utkatasana.
The sages were tricksters to name
      this odd shape Fierce Pose!
"The physical form doesn't seem to fit the name." I thought.
But bent upon not being fooled by the sages
      and their trickster ways,
I struck the pose again and again
      and went on the hunt for fierceness!

I learned why the beautiful Zig-Zag shape got its name
      and this brought me rewards galore!

By squatting down in earnest,
using my lower body to commune with the earth,
I attained fierce leg strength like a centaur
      running free in the wild.

By shooting my arms up
      as if to pierce the sky dome itself,
I gained a taste for the fierce nothingness of the void
      and began wondering what is
           beyond all knowing.

By visualizing my body as a lightning bolt
    charged with awakened Vitality,
I gained the mind control of a yogi
    and knew bliss from my anchored feet
        to my fingernails that blazed like fire.

I learned to think of the whole world,
with all its miraculous inhabitants,
as a singularly perfect web woven together by
    sacred relatedness.

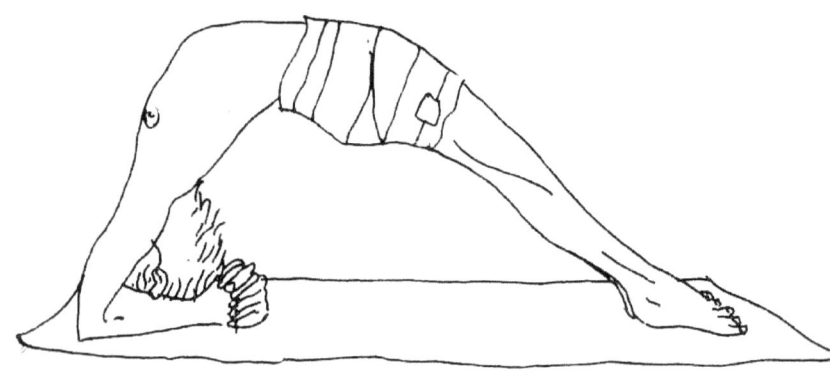

41

Last night I fell in love with the moon.
There was no helping it.
I looked up at the black night sky
      and saw a glowing sliver of light
           warm and welcoming.
I thought to myself:
"Hello Friend!
I want to be like You.
No darkness can intimidate me."

42

A student climbs up to the mountain cave retreat
        and asks the teacher:
"What is the meaning of life?"

The teacher says,
"There's good news and bad news.
First,
the bad news.
Your worst fears are confirmed.
All your hand wringing,
teeth gnashing,
strivings,
pure efforts,
earnest attempts to attain purity or oneness
        can't change this truth:
Life is meaningless and it doesn't matter what you do."

The student is crestfallen.
The inner pain and anguish are written on her body.
Her eyes grow a bit dimmer.
Her jaw sets a little more firmly and she steels herself
        to face the grim reality of the cruel world.

The teacher smiles a half smile,
winks a half wink,
and says,
"*Now,*
the good news.
Life is meaningless and it doesn't matter what you do.
So go play,
go kick butt,
stir it up,
do whatever causes you to burn and
*   light up this world like the sun and moon.*
Make the best of every day you are alive.
Play fearlessly and mean it.
Go all in.
Hold nothing back.
You've got nothing to gain
*   but you've also got nothing to lose."*

43

Practice really is marvelously simple
    when I finally let go of almost everything.
My needs are few now.
Just let me commune with earth,
water,
fire,
air,
and space.

Let me strike Tree Pose under the vast sky dome,
surrounded by space,
touched by the wind,
lit up by the Pillar of Fire that is my core,
and stand immovable merged
    with the abundant earth.

I scarcely need this body for asana
    or anything at all anymore.

Consciousness alone satisfies.

44

Do you have a definition of practice that you like?
Yes!
Ecstatic discipline.

45

They say yoga is calming your mind
    by sitting and meditating.
But this is no ordinary sitting.

No!

Yoga is:
electrified sitting,
animated bones sitting,
love sitting,
hate sitting,
joy sitting,
grief sitting,
sadness sitting,
rage sitting,
apathy sitting,
fear sitting,
courage sitting,
smallness sitting,
bigness sitting,
yearning sitting,
inner quest sitting,
searching for dharma sitting,
reaching infinitely sitting,
knowing no limits sitting,

farther and farther in to meet unity sitting,
all knowing sitting,
satisfied desire sitting,
embracing all states sitting,
neutrality sitting,
dispassionate sitting,
void sitting,
sitting at the foot of the world mountain sitting…
      Heck…
Becoming the world mountain sitting!

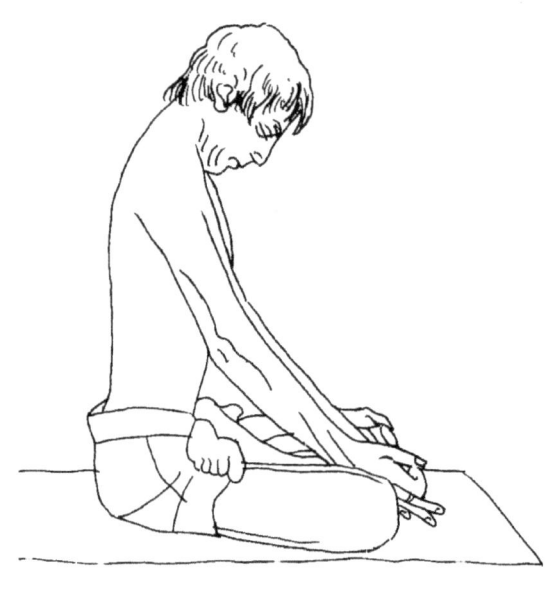

46

I am my own best friend.

I am not showing off when I say this.
It is a wondrous fact that I like my own company.

Me and my cast of inner characters
      get along quite well and it all
           comes from working as a team
                devoting ourselves to Hatha yoga.

I am shy to say it but I will overcome my shyness
      and my fear of sounding like a braggart
           to alert you to this worthy goal:
practice to become your own best friend
      and you'll experience true delight
           during your brief ride here.

www.ingramcontent.com/pod-product-compliance
Lightning Source LLC
Chambersburg PA
CBHW062150100526
44589CB00014B/1767